Practical
Pre-School

Planning for Learning through Recycling

by Rachel Sparks Linfield Illustrated by Cathy Hughes

Contents

Published by Step Forward Publishing Limited
St Jude's Church, Dulwich Road, Herne Hill, London, SE24 0PB Tel. 020 7738 5454
© Step Forward Publishing Limited 2007 www.practicalpreschool.com

Planning for Learning through Recycling ISBN: 978 1 904 575 139

Making plans

Why plan?

The purpose of planning is to make sure that all children enjoy a broad and balanced curriculum. All planning should be useful. Plans are working documents that you spend time preparing, which later should repay your efforts. Try to be concise. This will help you to find information quickly when you need it.

Long-term plans

Preparing a long-term plan, which maps out the curriculum during a year or even two, will help you to ensure that you are providing a variety of activities and are meeting the Statutory Framework for the Early Years Foundation Stage (2007).

Your long-term plan need not be detailed. Divide the time period over which you are planning into fairly equal sections such as half terms. Choose a topic for each section. Young children benefit from making links between the new ideas they encounter so as you select each topic, think about the time of year in which you plan to do it. A topic about minibeasts will not be very successful in November!

Although each topic will address all the learning areas, some could focus on a specific area. For example, a topic on Recycling would lend itself well to activities relating to creative development and knowledge and understanding of the world.

Another topic might particularly encourage the appreciation of stories. Try to make sure that you provide a variety of topics in your long-term plans such as:

Autumn 1	Nursery Rhymes
Autumn 2	Autumn/Christmas
Spring 1	Food
Spring 2	Weather
Summer 1	Recycling
Summer 2	Farming

Medium-term plans

Medium-term plans will outline the contents of a topic in a little more detail. One way to start this process is by brainstorming on a large piece of paper. Work with your team writing down all the activities you can think of which are relevant to the topic. As you do this it may become clear that some activities go well together. Think about dividing them into themes. The topic of 'Recycling', for example, has themes such as 'What can we recycle?', 'Recycling paper', 'Recycling boxes', Recycling plastic', 'Recycling clothes' and 'Recycling toys'. At this stage it is helpful to make a chart.

Write the theme ideas down the side of the chart and put a different area of learning at the top of each column. Now you can insert your brainstormed ideas and will quickly see where there are gaps. As you complete the chart take account of children's earlier experiences and provide opportunities for them to progress.

Refer back to the Statutory Framework for the Early Years Foundation Stage and check that you have addressed as many different aspects of it as you can. Once all your medium-term plans are complete make sure that there are no neglected areas.

Day-to-day plans

The plans you make for each day will outline aspects such as:

- resources needed;
- the way in which you might introduce activities;
- individual needs;
- the organisation of adult help;
- size of the group;
- timing;
- safety;
- key vocabulary.

Identify the learning and the ELGs that each activity is intended to promote. Make a note of any assessments or observations that you are likely to carry out. After carrying out the activities, make notes on your plans to say what was particularly successful, or any changes you would make another time.

A final note

Planning should be seen as flexible. Not all groups meet every day, and not all children attend every day. Any part of the plan can be used independently, stretched over a longer period or condensed to meet the needs of any group. You will almost certainly adapt the activities as children

Making plans

respond to them in different ways and bring their own ideas, interests and enthusiasms. The important thing is to ensure that the children are provided with a varied and enjoyable curriculum that meets their individual developing needs.

Using the book

- Collect or prepare suggested resources as listed on page 21.
- Read the section which outlines links to the Early Learning Goals (pages 4 - 7) and explains the rationale for the topic of 'Recycling'.
- For each weekly theme two activities are described in detail as an example to help you in your planning and preparation. Key vocabulary, questions and learning opportunities are identified.
- The skills chart on page 23 will help you to see at a glance which aspects of children's development are being addressed as a focus each week.
- As children take part in the topic activities, their learning will progress. Collecting Evidence on page 22 explains how you might monitor children's achievements.
- Find out on page 20 how the topic can be brought together in a 'grand finale' involving carers, children and friends.
- There is additional material to support the working partnership of families and children in the form of a Home Links page, and a photocopiable Parent's Page found at the back of the book.

It is important to appreciate that the ideas presented in this book will only be a part of your planning. Many activities that will be taking place as routine in your group may not be mentioned. For example, it is assumed that sand, dough, water, puzzles, floor toys and large scale apparatus are part of the ongoing pre-school experience, as are the opportunities for children to develop ICT skills.

Role-play areas, stories, rhymes, singing, and group discussion times are similarly assumed to be happening in each week although they may not be a focus for described activities. Groups should also ensure that there is a balance of adult led and child-initiated activities.

Throughout the topic on 'Recycling' encourage the children to understand what is meant by 'recycling' and its importance, both for themselves and the wider world. Where possible recycle materials for the topic. For example, painting, writing and drawing could be done on paper/card that is clean on one side but has had a previous use. Clean yogurt pots, margarine tubs etc make useful water tray toys or paint/glue pots.

Using the 'Early Learning Goals'

Having chosen your topic and made your medium-term plans you can use the Statutory Framework for the Early Years Foundation Stage to highlight the key learning opportunities your activities will address. The Early Learning Goals are split into six areas: Personal, Social and Emotional Development; Communication, Language and Literacy; Problem Solving, Reasoning and Numeracy; Knowledge and Understanding of the World; Physical Development and Creative Development. Do not expect each of your topics to cover every goal but your long-term plans should allow for all of them to be addressed by the time a child enters Year 1.

The following section highlights the Early Learning Goals in point form to show what children are expected to be able to do in each area of learning by the time they enter Year 1. These points will be used throughout this book to show how activities for a topic on 'Recycling' link to these expectations. For example Personal, Social and Emotional Development point 7 is 'form good relationships with peers and adults'. Activities suggested which provide the opportunity for children to do this will have the reference PS7. This will enable you to see which parts of the Early Learning Goals are covered in a given week and to plan for areas to be revisited and developed.

In addition you can ensure that activities offer variety in the goals to be encountered. Often an activity may be carried out to achieve different Early Learning Goals. For example, during this topic children make a giant patchwork of materials that can be recycled. Children will be using creative skills as they select colours, textures and shapes. In addition, they will develop knowledge and understanding of the world as they notice similarities and differences in the pieces they select and problem solving, reasoning and numeracy skills as they recognise shapes and count them. It is important, therefore, that activities have clearly defined goals so that these may be emphasised during the activity and for recording purposes.

Personal, Social and Emotional Development (PS)

This area of learning covers important aspects of development that affect the way children learn, behave and relate to others. By the end of the Early Years Foundation Stage (EYFS) children should:

PS1 Continue to be interested, excited and motivated to learn.

PS2 Be confident to try activities, initiate ideas and speak in a familiar group.

PS3 Maintain attention, concentrate and sit quietly when appropriate.

PS4 Respond to significant experiences, showing a range of feelings when appropriate.

PS5 Have a developing awareness of their own needs, views and feelings, and be sensitive to the needs, views and feelings of others.

PS6 Have a developing respect for their own cultures and beliefs and those of other people.

PS7 Form good relationships with adults and peers.

PS8 Work as a part of a group or class, taking turns and sharing fairly, understanding that there needs

to be agreed values and codes of behaviour for groups of people, including adults and children, to work together harmoniously.

PS9   Understand what is right, what is wrong and why.

PS10   Consider the consequences of their words and actions for themselves and others.

PS11   Dress and undress independently and mange their own personal hygiene.

PS12   Select and use activities and resources independently.

PS13   Understand that people have different needs, views, cultures and beliefs, that need to be treated with respect.

PS14   Understand that they can expect others to treat their needs, views, cultures and beliefs with respect.

The topic of 'Recycling' offers many opportunities for children's personal, social and emotional development. Times spent discussing what we can recycle will encourage children to speak in a group, to be interested and to consider consequences.

Through considering why we recycle the children will begin to understand what is wrong, what is right and why. Many of the areas outlined above, though, will be covered on an almost incidental basis as children carry out the activities described in this book for the other areas of children's learning. During undirected free choice times they will be developing PS5 whilst any small group activity that involves working with an adult will help children to work towards PS7.

Communication, Language and Literacy (L)

By the end of the EYFS, children should:

L1   Interact with others, negotiating plans and activities and taking turns in conversation.

L2   Enjoy listening to and using spoken and written language, and readily turn to it in their play and learning.

L3   Sustain attentive listening, responding to what they have heard with relevant comments, questions or actions.

L4   Listen with enjoyment, and respond to stories, songs and other music, rhymes and poems and make up their own stories, songs, rhymes and poems.

L5   Extend their vocabulary, exploring the meanings and sounds of new words.

L6   Speak clearly and audibly with confidence and control and show awareness of the listener.

L7   Use language to imagine and recreate roles and experiences.

L8   Use talk to organise, sequence and clarify thinking, ideas, feelings and events.

L9   Hear and say sounds in words in the order in which they occur.

L10   Link sounds to letters, naming and sounding the letters of the alphabet.

L11   Use their phonic knowledge to write simple regular words and make phonetically plausible attempts at more complex words.

L12   Explore and experiment with sounds, words and texts.

L13   Retell narratives in the correct sequence, drawing on language patterns of stories.

L14   Read a range of familiar and common words and simple sentences independently.

L15   Know that print carries meaning and, in English, is read from left to right and top to bottom.

L16   Show an understanding of the elements of stories, such as main character, sequence of events and openings, and how information can be found in non-fiction texts to answer questions about where, who, why and how.

L17   Attempt writing for different purposes, using features of different forms such as lists, stories and instructions.

L18   Write their own names and other things such as labels and captions, and begin to form simple sentences, sometimes using punctuation.

L19   Use a pencil and hold it effectively to form recognisable letters, most of which are correctly formed.

A number of the activities suggested for the theme of 'Recycling' encourage the children to write using their phonic knowledge and to recognise words. They have the opportunity to produce posters, write labels, make 'We can recycle' books and work in a role-play office.

Activities, based on well known picture books and stories, allow the children to enjoy sharing the books and to respond in a variety of ways to what they hear, reinforcing and extending their vocabularies. Throughout all the activities the children are encouraged to interact and to listen.

Problem Solving, Reasoning and Numeracy (N)

By the end of the EYFS, children should:

N1   Say and use number names in order in familiar contexts.

N2   Count reliably up to ten everyday objects.

N3   Recognise numerals 1 to 9.

N4   Use developing mathematical ideas and methods to solve practical problems.

N5   In practical activities and discussion, begin to use the vocabulary involved in adding and subtracting

N6   Use language such as 'more' or 'less' to compare two numbers.

N7   Find one more or one less than a number from one to ten.

N8   Begin to relate addition to combining two groups of objects and subtraction to 'taking away'.

N9   Use language such as 'greater', 'smaller', 'heavier' or 'lighter' to compare quantities.

N10   Talk about, recognise and recreate simple patterns

N11   Use language such as 'circle' or 'bigger' to describe the shape and size of solids and flat shapes.

N12   Use everyday words to describe position.

The theme of 'Recycling' provides a meaningful context for activities that encourage the children to use numbers, to reason and to solve problems.

The opportunity to count occurs as children use the 'Socks in a tub' number rhyme, sing 'Ten plastic bottles to recycle' and count objects that they sort according to the material from which they were made.

Children will explore shapes and size as they collaborate to make towers with boxes and yogurt pots and turn cereal boxes inside out. Children have the chance to use mathematical language as they compare amounts, shapes and numbers.

Knowledge and Understanding of the World (K)

By the end of the EYFS, children should:

K1   Investigate objects and materials by using all of their senses as appropriate.

K2   Find out about, and identify, some features of living things, objects and events they observe.

K3   Look closely at similarities, differences, patterns and change.

K4   Ask questions about why things happen and how things work.

K5   Build and construct with a wide range of objects, selecting appropriate resources and adapting their work where necessary.

K6   Select the tools and techniques they need to shape, assemble and join materials they are using.

K7   Find out about and identify the uses of everyday technology and use information and communication technology and programmable toys to support their learning.

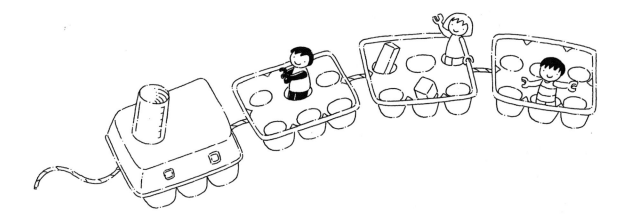

K8   Find out about past and present events in their own lives, and in those of their families and other people they know.

K9   Observe, find out about and identify features in the place they live and the natural world.

K10   Find out about their environment, and talk about those features they like and dislike.

K11   Begin to know about their own cultures and beliefs and those of other people.

The topic of 'Recycling' offers many opportunities for children to make observations, to ask questions and to compare. As they explore packaging and recycle paper they are encouraged to notice details. Activities such as 'change a bottle' and making models and vehicles give them the opportunity to select materials and to construct.

Through all the activities children should be encouraged to observe, to talk and to give reasons for choices and observations.

Physical Development (PD)

By the end of the EYFS, children should:

PD1   Move with confidence, imagination and in safety.
PD2   Move with control and coordination.
PD3   Travel around, under, over and through balancing and climbing equipment.
PD4   Show awareness of space, of themselves and of others.
PD5   Recognise the importance of keeping healthy, and those things which contribute to this.
PD6   Recognise the changes that happen to their bodies when they are active.
PD7   Use a range of small and large equipment.
PD8   Handle tools, objects, construction and malleable materials safely and with increasing control.

Activities such as using dough and construction toys will offer experience of PD8. Through pretending to travel to and visit a recycling centre, children will have the opportunity to move with control and imagination.

When using a range of small equipment, such as beanbags and sock balls, and following a path made of recycle symbol arrows the children will be encouraged to develop their co-ordination and control.

Creative Development (C)

By the end of the EYFS, children should:

C1   Respond in a variety of ways to what they see, hear, smell, touch and feel.

C2   Express and communicate their ideas, thoughts and feelings by using a widening range of materials, suitable tools, imaginative and role-play, movement, designing and making, and a variety of songs and musical instruments.

C3   Explore colour, texture, shape, form and space in two or three dimensions.

C4   Recognise and explore how sounds can be changed, sing simple songs from memory, recognise repeated sounds and sound patterns and match movements to music.

C5   Use their imagination in art and design, music, dance, imaginative and role-play and stories.

During this topic children will experience working with a variety of materials as they make collages using recycled materials. They will be able to develop their imaginations and skills of painting and colour mixing as they paint self portraits and book characters wearing recycled clothes.

Throughout all the activities children should be encouraged to talk about what they see and feel as they communicate their ideas in painting, models, collage work and role-play. When using instruments made from recycled pots and boxes the children will recognise and explore how sounds can be changed.

Week 1

What can we recycle?

Personal, Social and Emotional Development

- Discuss with the children what recycling is. Explain that one meaning is to reuse materials and objects that might otherwise be thrown away, either as they are or in a changed form. Show children some packaging and ask for ideas of how it could be reused. Talk about why recycling is important. (PS1, 9)
- Make a display of recycled objects such as a comb made from recycled bottles or a pencil case made from recycled tyres. Ask the children to try to bring in other recycled objects. (PS1, 4)

Communication, Language and Literacy

- Make posters to label boxes for collecting items to be used during the topic such as different types of paper; plastic bottles and cartons; unwanted toys; books and clothes etc. (L17, 18, 19)
- Help to write letters to carers requesting items to use in 'book bags' in Week 6 (see activity opposite). (L15, 19)
- Make a group 'big book' about recycling. Use catalogues and magazines to find pictures to illustrate the book. Also, stick in pieces of recyclable materials. (L3, 5)

Problem Solving, Reasoning and Numeracy

- Show the children a recycling symbol made up from arrows (the Internet or packaging can provide examples). Make repeating patterns with arrows cut from a variety of colours of paper. (N10)
- Sort clean packaging, using the recycling symbol, into things that can and cannot be recycled. Count the number in each set. (N1, 2)
- Set out toy bricks and small boxes as areas in a recycling centre. On cards write/draw labels for the different areas such as garden waste, paper, electrical goods etc. Use everyday words to explain to the children where you would like them to drive toy lorries and cars, deliver items and park. (N12)

Knowledge and Understanding of the World

- Examine cans to find the recycle sign. Use magnets to sort cans into ones made from aluminium (not

attracted by a magnet) and ones made out of steel (attracted by a magnet). (NB If using empty cans ensure they are clean and that there are no sharp edges. (K1, 2)
- Provide lolly sticks and other scrap materials for the children to enjoy designing and making 'something useful' (e.g. a table for a doll; a star to be a decoration; a flag to label a plant pot). Encourage the children to explain what they have made and to evaluate whether their constructions are useful. (K5, 6)
- Look through a bin of clean rubbish. Talk about which bits could be recycled. (K1)
- Discuss how things are recycled in the local environment. Help the children to be aware of composting bins, bottle banks etc. (K9)

Physical Development

- Put out three buckets labeled with pictures of a tennis ball, a plastic ball and a beanbag. Talk about the importance, when taking some items to a recycling centre, of sorting by material. Encourage the children to enjoy aiming a variety of balls and beanbags into the correct buckets. (PD7)

- Tell a story of a visit to a recycling centre. Encourage the children to mime to the words. Invite suggestions for things to take to the centre and also for things they might like to find there, to use. (PD1)
- Remind children of the recycling symbol. Use chalk to mark out a cyclical trail, of arrows, for the children to move along. Give instructions for ways to move. (PD2, 4)

Creative Development

- Make a giant patchwork collage of different materials that could be recycled. (C3)
- Invite the children to enjoy using a role-play recycling centre (see activity opposite). (C5)
- Look at recycling symbols. On black paper paint colourful arrows. (C3)

Activity: Writing book bag letters

Learning opportunity: Helping to write letters about the book bags.

Early learning goal: Communication, Language and Literacy. Children should know that print carries meaning and, in English, is read from left to right and top to bottom. They should use a pencil and hold it effectively to form recognisable letters, most of which are correctly formed.

Resources: An A3 sized version of the book bag letter and an A4 copy for each child; pencils, example non-fiction and fiction book bags (e.g. book on insects or dinosaurs and plastic models; a version of 'Goldilocks and the three bears', three teddies and a fair haired doll).

Key vocabulary: Fiction, non-fiction, book bag.

Organisation: Whole group introduction, small group activity.

What to do: Explain that the group hopes to have a collection of book bags that can be borrowed to take home. Show the example bags and how the bears and doll can be used to retell the tale of 'Goldilocks and the Three Bears'. Look at the plastic models and use the non-fiction book to identify them. Talk about what will need to be collected. Tell the group that the idea is to recycle books, bags etc. Nothing is to be bought. Show the children the large letter pointing to the words as it is read aloud. Invite each child to decorate an A4 letter, to fill in their carers' names and to sign it.

Dear _____,
As part of our topic on 'recycling' we are hoping to make some 'book bags'. Each bag will have a book and something to use like puppets, dolls, soft toys; plastic models, a game or jigsaw. On the attached sheet is a list of things that we would like to collect to go with books that we already have. We would also really like to collect more books, things to go with them and book-sized, sealable bags. If you can help us, please send in your donations by _____.
With many thanks,
From _____.

Activity: In the recycling centre

Learning opportunity: Enjoying role-play in a recycling centre.

Early learning goal: Creative Development. Children should use their imagination in role-play.

Resources: Role-play recycling centre containing large plastic boxes labeled for items useful for making models such as boxes, cardboard tubes, plastic bottles and tubs, fabric, papers, shiny things etc.; a table with a phone and writing materials; a cash register, play money and receipt pad; fluorescent coloured tabards; catalogues with furniture, electrical goods etc.

Key vocabulary: Recycle, names for materials, please, thank you.

Organisation: Small groups of up to four children.

What to do: Talk to the children about the different types of rubbish that families produce. Talk about the things that if left, would rot and the things that would not. Talk about the things that could be re-used without change, and ones like newspaper that could be recycled. Remind the children of why it is important to recycle.

Put on a fluorescent tabard and take on the role of someone who works in the recycle centre. Invite a child to come with a bag of things to recycle. Show them where to put the things. Answer the phone and model a conversation with someone who is looking for a bike. Describe possible ones. Ask the child to take on the worker role and invite another child to visit the centre. Encourage the worker to sort, to tidy, to answer the phone and also to sell furniture, electrical items etc cut from a catalogue.

Over the week, use the centre both for role-play and, also, to find recyclable resources for activities.

Display

Cut out the letters in 'We can recycle' for a title, from large pieces of cereal packet and provide scrap papers for the children to decorate the letters. Cover a display board with plain wallpaper. Put up a border to link with the colours in the letters and arrange them in the centre of the board. Around the letters display objects or pictures of them to show what can be recycled. On a table arrange the recycled objects brought in by the children. Involve the children in choosing paper for mounting their patterns that are based on the recycling symbol. Display them on a board with a border of paper arrows.

Week 2
Recycling paper

Personal, Social and Emotional Development

- Explain to the children how paper is made. Talk about the age trees need to be before they are cut down. Encourage the children to understand the importance of recycling paper for saving trees. (PS3)
- Look through a wastepaper bin of clean rubbish. Sort out all the paper. Ask which bits of the paper could have been used for something else (e.g. Paper that is clean on one side for pictures or writing; coloured scraps for collages etc.) Invite each child to select some of the paper and reuse it. (PS12)

Communication, Language and Literacy

- Make 'I can recycle ...' books from paper that has been used on one side (see activity opposite). (L11, 18)
- Set out an area as a post office or an office with scrap paper, used envelopes, junk mail envelopes etc. Encourage the children to use the areas for writing and role-play. (L7, 17)
- Share one of the 'Jolly Postman' type books, by Janet and Allan Ahlberg (Heinemann), with the children. As a group, make a similar book by recycling envelopes and greetings cards. (L4)

Problem Solving, Reasoning and Numeracy

- Use scrap paper to do simple origami such as aeroplanes, boats, hats and tulips. As the children work encourage them to describe the shapes they are folding. (N11)
- Use patterned wallpaper or pieces of used wrapping paper to play 'I spy'. Use details of the patterns, shapes, positions, quantities and sizes to give clues. (N10, 11, 12)
- Make a triangular shaped hat from a piece of newspaper and invite a child to wear it. Sing 'Child's name's hat it has three corners' to the tune of 'My hat it has three corners' in *Okki-tokki-unga Action Songs for Children* chosen by Beatrice Harrop, Linda Friend and David Gadsby. Repeat the song changing the child's name and the number of corners. Ask the chosen child to hold up their fingers to show the number of corners or to point to the number on a number line. (N1, 2, 3)

Knowledge and Understanding of the World

- Make a collection of recycled papers for children to compare with paper that has not been recycled. Encourage them to notice both similarities and differences. (K1, 3)
- Recycle newspaper by tearing it into small pieces, pulling it apart in water to pulp it and, when ready, pressing it onto a plastic lid. When dry, encourage the children to compare their recycled paper with newspaper. (K3, 4)
- Fill a large, clean container (e.g. empty sand or water tray) with shredded scrap paper. Hide objects within the tray. Invite the children in turn, to find by feeling two objects and to say how they are similar and how they are different. (K3)

Physical Development

- Play the 'Paper Collection Game' (see activity opposite). (PD7, 8)
- Play the flapping fish game. Place a hoop in the centre of a large space. Use magazines to waft fish cut from newspaper into the hoop. (PD7, 8)

Creative Development

- Make fruit and vegetables from papier mâché, for use in a role-play shop in Week 3. (C3)
- Make collages of butterflies from coloured scraps of paper torn from magazines. (C3)
- Enjoy painting on papers taken from the recycle bin. (C3, 5)

Activity: Making recycling books

Learning opportunity: Making books and attempting to write simple words.

Early learning goal: Communication, Language and Literacy. Children should use their phonic knowledge to write simple regular words and make phonetically plausible attempts at more complex words. They should use a pencil

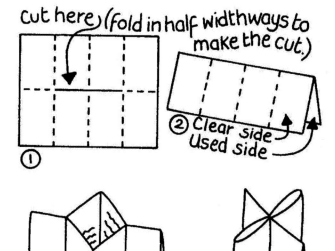

cut here)(fold in half widthways to make the cut.)

① ② Clear side / Used side ③ ④

and hold it effectively to form recognisable letters, most of which are correctly formed.

Resources: A4 sized scrap paper that is clean on one side; scissors, pencils, crayons, example of a folded book.

Key vocabulary: Fold, half, again, book, recycle.

Organisation: Small groups.

What to do: Show the children the example book. Explain that it has been made with paper that is only clean on one side. Give a sheet of paper to each child and, demonstrating each stage, help them to fold a book.
Explain that the books will be about recycling. Help the children to write the title 'I can recycle' and their names on the covers. Ask the children to draw/stick pictures of things that can be recycled in their books. If appropriate, encourage the children to label the pictures.

Activity: The Paper Collection Game

Learning opportunity: Developing fine motor skills whilst enjoying playing a game.

Early learning goal: Physical Development. Children should use a range of small equipment. They will handle objects with increasing control.

Resources: Paper squares of side 10 – 15cm; for each child a knotted shoelace; a sand timer (e.g. 60 seconds).

Key vocabulary: Recycle, square, collect.

Organisation: Small groups within a large space.

What to do: Remind the children of why it is important to recycle paper. Talk about the way some groups collect paper, to be recycled, to raise money. Explain that they are going to play the Paper Collection Game.

Lay out squares of scrap paper. Give each child a shoe lace, knotted at one end. Demonstrate how to pick up a piece of paper and thread it, through the centre, on to the shoelace. Challenge them to see how many squares they can thread onto their laces before the sand runs through a timer. Finish by counting the number of pieces that have been collected.

(Note: The game could also be used for number recognition or phonics activities. Numbers/letters can be written on squares and children can be challenged to collect squares for a given number or word.)

Display

Involve the children in mounting their collages and paintings by using paper that has previously been used as backing paper for another display. Help them to write titles and their names to label the pictures. Cover a table with fabric and display the 'I can recycle' books. Nearby put out a basket of objects containing objects made from paper and other materials for the children to sort into hoops according to what they are made from.

Week 3

Recycling boxes

Personal, Social and Emotional Development
- Show the children one box. As a group, make a list of all the ways that it could be used. Encourage the children to be imaginative. (PS2)
- Make promise boxes (see activity opposite). (PS10)

Communication, Language and Literacy
- Ask the children to have a book search for ones that include a picture of a box (e.g. *A Dark, Dark Tale* by Ruth Brown; *Dear Zoo* by Rod Campbell; *Harry and the Bucketful of Dinosaurs* or *Harry and the Robots* by Ian Whybrow; *Mog's Box* by Helen Nicholl and Jan Pieńkowski). Enjoy sharing the books. Encourage the children to retell the stories by using the pictures. (L4)
- Use cereal packets or shoe boxes labeled with 'at', 'og', 'it', 'en' and 'ig' to collect rhyming words. Encourage the children to write words on pieces of card and post them into the boxes. Use the words for sorting activities and to make simple rhymes. (L9, 11, 12)

Problem Solving, Reasoning and Numeracy
- Use shoe boxes, coloured cubes and cards with the numbers up to 10 written on for sorting and counting activities. (N1, 2, 3, 6)
- Use cereal packets, shoe boxes etc for building towers. Encourage the children to use words such as 'taller/shorter than'; 'wider', 'narrow' etc to describe the towers that they make. (N9)
- Use large and small boxes, filled with the papier mâché fruits and vegetables made in week 2, for a role-play green grocer's shop. Encourage the children to be both the cashier and the customer. Enjoy buying and selling for amounts up to 10 pence. (N1, 2, 5)
- Involve the children in turning cereal packets inside out in readiness for craft activities (see activity opposite). (N11)

Knowledge and Understanding of the World
- Use folded card from cereal packets and large boxes to make chutes for rolling small balls. Help the children to investigate which chute lets a ball roll the furthest. (K3, 4)
- Use the cereal packets that the children remade, inside out. Challenge them to turn the boxes into vehicles. Encourage the children to think how to give them wheels that turn. Use ICT to give each vehicle a number plate. (K6, 7)
- Make a collection of boxes that are used for different purposes. Sort the boxes according to different criteria such as size, strength, type of card, way they are opened, use etc. Encourage the children to give reasons for why a box is good/bad for its particular purpose and to consider whether the box is necessary. (K2, 3)

Physical Development
- Use large cardboard boxes, as walls, to mark out a path. Enjoy rolling and dribbling large and small balls along the path in between the walls. (PD2, 7)
- Practise throwing balls of different sizes into boxes. Write numbers on the boxes and challenge the children to throw that number of things in. (PD7)
- Practise kicking large balls into a large box lying on its side. (PD7)

Creative Development
- Make patchworks from tessellating shapes such as hexagons and squares, of side length about 5cm, cut from colourful cereal packets, biscuit/cake boxes etc. (C3)

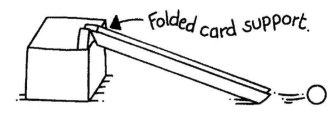

Folded card support.

Folded + taped card to support the chute on the box.

- Use large boxes to make a puppet theatre. Invite the children to choose a puppet and to make up plays with their peers. (C5)
- Make jewelry boxes by decorating small boxes with sequins, shells and scrap materials. Provide card circles cut from cereal packets to decorate as necklaces, badges or brooches. (C3)

Activity: Making promise boxes

Learning opportunity: Talking about promises and feelings.

Early learning goal: Personal, Social and Emotional Development. Children should consider the consequences of their words and actions for themselves and others.

Resources: An example promise box, pencils, crayons, for each child a small box and small pieces of card.

Key vocabulary: Promise, box.

Organisation: Whole group introduction, small groups for the activity.

What to do: Talk to the children about promises and what it means if someone says 'I promise'. Show the children a small box that has been decorated with stickers, sequins etc. From the box take out a piece of paper that says 'I promise that I will hang up my coat each day on the peg.' Ask why this promise is helpful. Ask for suggestions of things that the children could promise to do that would be helpful at home or within the group. Invite pairs of children to decorate boxes and to write or draw two promises on small pieces of card. Return to the boxes a week later to see whether the children have managed to keep their promises.

Activity: Turning boxes inside out

Learning opportunity: Talking about shapes and their properties.

Early learning goal: Problem Solving, Reasoning and Numeracy. Use language such as 'circle' or 'bigger' to describe the shape and size of solids and flat shapes.

Resources: Masking tape, scissors and for each child a cereal packet or box from biscuits.

Key vocabulary: Shape, rectangle, square, side, face, corner, box, cuboid.

Organisation: Small group.

What to do: Show the group the boxes. Encourage them to notice their similarities and differences. Talk about the shapes of each face. Count the number of faces for each box and, also, the number of sides for each 2-d shaped face.

Demonstrate how to open the box out and to refold it, inside out, into a box with clean faces. Remake the box using masking tape. Show the children how they can anchor the end of the masking tape on the table, hold the reel in one hand and cut with their other. Ask each child to select a box to turn inside out. Explain that they will use the box later in the week to make a vehicle. As they work, encourage them to talk about the sizes of the boxes and to use the correct names for the shapes, faces etc.

Display

On a table put out the box and ideas list from the first activity. Over the week encourage the children to use the box for role-play and, also, to think up more uses for the box. Display the jewelry boxes on a table covered with black paper. Involve the children in the making of a sign to say 'Please do not touch'. Explain that when the boxes go home the paper will be re-used in another activity or display. Put up the card patchworks as a giant collage. Outline each piece with black, border strip paper.

Week 4

Recycling plastic

Personal, Social and Emotional Development
- Use yogurt pots, margarine tubs etc. to hold the paint, water and glue during creative activities. Help the children to realise that the pots are being recycled. (PS12)
- Show children a collection of thin, plastic carriers and, also, 'bags for life'. Discuss why the 'bags for life' are a good idea. (NB For safety, ensure all the bags have safety holes and that no child attempts to place a bag over their head.) (PS9, 10)

Communication, Language and Literacy
- Talk about sending messages in a bottle. Encourage each child to 'write' a message for another child and place it in a small plastic bottle. Float the bottles in a water tray and invite each child to select one bottle. (L11, 18)
- Make whiteboards from either laminated scrap paper or card in clear plastic wallets. Let the children enjoy practising to write on their recycled, plastic white boards. (L11)
- Use a permanent pen to write the letters from the children's names on milk bottle plastic screw-on lids. Let the children find their own letters to spell their names and, also, use the lids to spell out new words. (L12)

Problem Solving, Reasoning and Numeracy
- Enjoy comparing the capacity of a variety of plastic pots, tubs and bottles in the sand or water trays.

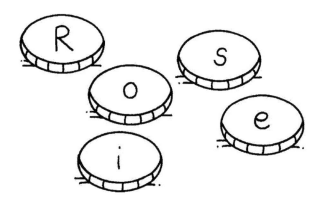

- Encourage the children to count the number of pots/tubs to fill various containers and arrange them in size order. (N2, 4, 9)
- Use the 'Ten plastic bottles' number rhyme (see activity opposite). (N1, 2, 7)
- Stick number labels from one to ten onto ten plastic pots. Use the pots to order numbers, to count on and back and for placing a given number of plastic objects into each pot. (N1, 2, 3)

Knowledge and Understanding of the World
- Enjoy planting seeds such as cress or apple pips in clean yogurt pots. (K2)
- Talk about the properties of plastic and the different ways that it can be used. Provide pieces of plastic carriers and scrap materials for the children to make waterproof shelters for a small toy. (K5, 6)
- Use plastic bottles as rain gauges. Record the rainfall over a couple of weeks. (K3)

Physical Development
- Use plastic bottles as skittles. (PD2, 7)
- Provide plastic balls, hoops and bottles for the children to invent and play their own games. (PD7)

Creative Development
- Challenge the children to turn a bottle into something else (see activity opposite). (C3)
- Use plastic bottles, yogurt pots, pretend credit cards, bottle lids (as money) and other recycled plastic objects in a role-play café. (C5)
- Turn plastic bottles, pots and tubs into musical instruments such as drums and shakers. Use the instruments to accompany the singing of favourite songs. (C4)
- Use the plastic lids from bottles and jars, and ready mixed paint to print 'feelings patterns' on strips of black paper. Encourage the children to choose the colours for a reason. E.g. Red and orange might be chosen as hot, happy or angry colours. Blue might mean sad or cold. (C2)

Plastic bottle cut to give funnel and collecting pot.

Activity: Counting with 'Ten plastic bottles'

Learning opportunity: Enjoying counting with a number song.

Early learning goal: Problem Solving, Reasoning and Numeracy. Children should say and use number names in order in familiar contexts; count reliably up to ten everyday objects and find one less than a number from one to ten.

Resources: A plastic recycled object (e.g. a comb) and an example of the object from which it was recycled (e.g. a vending machine plastic beaker).

Key vocabulary: Recycled, plastic, names of the recycled objects.

Organisation: Whole group

What to do: Show the group the recycled object. Talk about how some plastic objects can be recycled to make new things. Make a list of objects that might be made from recycled plastic. To the tune of 'Ten green bottles' sing 'Ten plastic bottles to recycle'.

10 plastic bottles to recycle,
10 plastic bottles to recycle,
And if one plastic bottle
Should be turned into a comb,
There'd be 9 plastic bottles to recycle.

For subsequent verses encourage the children to show the number of bottles with their fingers and to make suggestions for the object made from recycled plastic.

On further occasions remove varying numbers of bottles each time.

Activity: Changing a bottle

Learning opportunity: Using the imagination to change a bottle.

Early learning goal: Creative Development. Children should explore colour, texture, shape, form and space in two or three dimensions.

Resources: Paper, pencils, scrap materials, masking tape, plastic bottles with lids, sand, paint, glue, scissors.

Key vocabulary: Recycle, change, bottle, names for the materials used and the models made.

Organisation: Small groups.

What to do: Introduce this activity one day and do it on another to give children time to think and plan.

Show the children a plastic bottle. Encourage them to observe it closely and to think of things that have a similar shape. Tell them that they cannot cut the bottle but can add things to it. Challenge them to give ideas of ways they could use the bottle to make a model. Help them to realise that the bottle could stand up, lay on its side etc. Ask them to draw their ideas.

Another day let the children select materials to make their models. Ones that stand up should include some sand to help them balance. If bottles are to be painted, they should first be covered with masking tape.

Display

Involve the children in finding appropriate backgrounds to display their bottle models. This could include finding toys, helping to make grass/roads/flowers etc and also, making labels and signs to ensure that people 'look with their eyes and not their hands'.

Write out the song '10 plastic bottles to recycle' on a large sheet of paper with the children's ideas for the recycled objects. Put this on a board with a table nearby for displaying the children's instruments.

Week 5

Recycling clothes

Personal, Social and Emotional Development

- Explain how to fold and take care of clothes. Place a variety of clothes in a home corner for the children to enjoy dressing, undressing and tidying away. (PS9, 11)
- Ask carers to donate or lend clothing suitable for fairytale role-play. Encourage the children to take turns in using the clothes and to work collaboratively. (PS8)
- Make a collection of unwanted baby clothes. Talk about the way babies change and grow. Use the clothes to dress baby dolls. (PS4)

Communication, Language and Literacy

- Enjoy sharing *The Smartest Giant in Town* by Julia Donaldson. Talk about all the items of clothing that the giant recycled. Provide clothes for the children to enjoy retelling and acting the story. (L4, 13)
- Enjoy looking through a selection of the children's favourite picture books. Provide a box of clothes for the children to select new outfits for one of the characters. Encourage the children to say why they think the character would like the clothing. (L4, 6)
- Make posters for a 'Nearly new clothing shop'. (17, 19)

Problem Solving, Reasoning and Numeracy

- Use the 'Socks rhyme' to solve problems about pairs (see activity opposite). (N2, 4)
- Make a number line by pegging up numbered items of clothing. Use the line for number identification, counting, adding and subtracting. Encourage the children also, to enjoy using the line during times of independent play. (N1, 2, 3, 5)
- Sort a box of unwanted shoes by their sizes. (N1, 2, 3)

Knowledge and Understanding of the World

- Recycle clean nylon tights to make grass heads. Cut about 30cm from a leg of a pair of tights, tie it at one end and turn it inside out. Put a handful of grass seed in, top with sawdust and tie the end with a knot. Soak the 'head' and then place it in a shallow dish of water. Encourage the children to look at the heads each day to ensure they are kept moist, whilst they wait for the 'hair' to grow. (K1, 2, 3)
- Explain to the children where wool and cotton come

from. Help the children to recognize different types of fabric. Use fabric scraps to make a whole group collage, patchwork hat and tunic for a scarecrow. (K6, 9)

Physical Development

- Use rolled up socks as balls. (PD7)
- In a safe, large space enjoy throwing an unwanted Wellington boot. Challenge the children to throw it as far as they can. (PD7)
- Tell a story in which children wake early to go out shopping for clothes in charity shops. Encourage them to listen carefully and to move to the words. If large equipment is available use it as bridges, tunnels etc for the children to travel to the shops. (PD1, 3, 4)

Creative Development

- Make 'sock buddies' (see activity opposite). (CD3, 5)
- Provide a box of unwanted clothes. Invite children to try them on and to paint self-portraits. (C3)
- Make sock puppets. Use them to tell stories. (C5)

Activity: Counting 'Socks in a tub'

Learning opportunity:
Using a number rhyme to make and count pairs.

Early learning goal: Problem Solving, Reasoning and Numeracy. Children should count reliably up to ten everyday objects. They should use developing mathematical ideas and methods to solve practical problems.

Resources: A basket containing six pairs of patterned/coloured socks – each pair must be different.

Key vocabulary: Pair, numbers to 12, jumble sale.

Organisation: Whole group sitting on the floor.

What to do: Show the group the basket containing six, loose socks. Explain that the socks have been washed ready to take to a jumble sale, but first they need to be sorted into pairs. Hand a sock out to each of six children. Count the number of socks. Recite the 'Socks in a tub' rhyme up to 'for people to use'. After this line ask the children to get into matching pairs. Count the number of pairs and recite the final line. Repeat the rhyme with different numbers of socks.

Rub a dub, dub,
6 socks in a tub.
How many pairs can we make?
Sort them in twos
For people to use.
There's 3 pairs ready to take.

On subsequent occasions, include odd numbers of socks. This will help the children to understand that 'pair' means 'two' and that the left over sock is not a 'pair'.

Activity: Making 'Sock Buddies'
Learning opportunity: Using socks to make people to use in role-play.

Early learning goal: Creative Development. Children should explore colour, texture, shape, form and space in two or three dimensions. They should use their imagination in art and design imaginative and role-play.

Resources: Clean, unwanted, ankle socks; rubber bands, stickers/eyes for decorating faces; tissue paper/kitchen roll; example sock buddy.

Key vocabulary: Recycle, sock, buddy.

Organisation: Small group.

What to do: Demonstrate how to make a sock buddy by:
1. Stuffing the foot with scrunched up tissue paper/kitchen roll to make a body. (The amount will depend on the size of sock and shape of buddy desired.)
2. Securing the body with an elastic band. (This makes a neck.)
3. Putting in more paper to make a head.
4. Securing the head by tying a knot in the sock or using another elastic band. The remaining sock material could be turned back to make a hat, trimmed as hair or left.
5. Using stickers/'wobbly eyes' to make facial features.

Use the buddies to tell stories and for role-play.

Display
Mount the portraits and display them with number labels. On a table put out A4 cards which list the children's names and small cards with numbers. Encourage the children to look at the display and match the children's names with the numbers for the portraits. Use plastic carrier bags to protect a table for displaying the grass heads. At floor height, put up the scarecrow clothes on a scarecrow cut from sugar paper. Encourage the children to look after the scarecrow as they 'read' stories to him, talk and give him 'food'.

Week 6

Recycling toys

Personal, Social and Emotional Development

- Talk about the importance of taking good care of toys. As a group sort the group's toys to check pieces are not missing, things are not broken etc. (PS9)
- Involve the children in making up book bags with the toys and books donated by carers, as a result of the letters written in Week 1. Explain how and when the book bags can be borrowed. Talk about the importance of checking that all the items are replaced back in the bags after their use. (PS9)

Communication, Language and Literacy

- Enjoy sharing any of the 'Old Bear' type stories by Jane Hissey. Encourage the children to imagine that the toys have been passed on to the group. As a group imagine what the toys would do. (L3, 4)
- Re-tell the story of 'Goldilocks and the three bears'. Discuss how the broken chair could be recycled (see activity opposite.) (L4)
- Enjoy using the book bags. (L4, 13)

Problem Solving, Reasoning and Numeracy

- Provide toy cars for the children to sort by colour and by size. Ask the children questions such as 'Are there more red cars or blue?'; 'Which car is the longest?' and 'If we had one more yellow car how many would we have altogether?' (N4, 5, 6)

- Use construction toys to make buildings and use language associated with shape, size and position. (N9, 11, 12)
- Show the children an example of a set of traditional Russian dolls that stack inside each other. Enjoy arranging the dolls in size order. Give each child a Russian doll shape cut from scrap card. Decorate the dolls with stickers in repeating patterns. Encourage the children to describe the patterns that they make. (10, 11)

Knowledge and Understanding of the World

- Make kites from straws, long pipe-cleaners, wool and newspaper (see activity opposite). (K5)
- Make a collection of safe, broken toys such as dolls that have lost a leg or arm, soft toys without facial features, toy cars that have lost wheels and, also, ones that have lost pieces such as jigsaws. Invite the children to select toys to mend, change and/or play with. (K6)
- Invite adults known to the group to show and talk about the toys they used to play with when they were children. (K8)

Physical Development

- Recycle yogurt pots with holes as bubble 'blowers'. Enjoy blowing bubbles, in a safe outside area, on a fine day. Ensure that each child has their own 'blower'. (PD7)
- Use recycled items (e.g. plastic lids from bottles, plastic toys that come free in breakfast cereals, lids from coffee jars) as cutters and for mark making in malleable materials. (PD8)

Creative Development

- Make a collection of unwanted clean, soft toys and dolls. Paint their portraits in readiness for the 'Bring and swap sale'. (C3)
- Involve the children in changing a role-play area such as a home or an office for a different use. Explain that as they are recycling, they are only allowed to use items from within their group room or can use scrap materials to make props. (C2)

● Use boxes and other scrap materials to make a toy zoo, safari park, town or farm. Alternatively, read *Harry and the Robots* by Ian Whybrow and make new robots for Harry. (C5)

Activity: Recycling for Goldilocks and the three bears

Learning opportunity: Responding to a familiar story.

Early learning goal: Communication, Language and Literacy. Children should listen with enjoyment, and respond to stories.

Resources: A version of 'Goldilocks and the Three bears'; flip chart, pen, a wooden chair.

Key vocabulary: Recycle, broken, mend, chair.

Organisation: Large or small group.

What to do: Read or tell the story of 'Goldilocks and the Three Bears'. Focus on the broken chair. Encourage the children to talk about how they would feel if Goldilocks had broken one of their possessions. Ask what Goldilocks could do to show she was sorry and discuss ways that the chair could have been recycled.

Explain that Goldilocks would like to send the bears a letter to show she is sorry but that she needs our help. She has asked the group to write the letter and to give ideas to the bears of what they could do with the chair pieces. As a group write a letter. Encourage the children to offer ideas and to help to spell some of the words.

Activity: Newspaper Kites

Learning opportunity: Making simple kites and experiencing pulls.

Early learning goal: Knowledge and Understanding of the World. Children should build and construct with a wide range of objects, selecting appropriate resources and adapting their work where necessary.

Resources: Wax crayons, tape, scissors, for each child: 2 bendy straws, 2 pipe-cleaners, a sheet of newspaper, 2 pieces of wool of about 30cm and 40 cm long, paper rectangles for the tail.

Key vocabulary: Kite, push, pull, newspaper, recycle.

Organisation: Small group.

What to do: Show the children a kite or picture of one. Talk to the children about kites and how they fly.

Help each child to push pipe cleaners through two bendy straws to form a kite frame. Give each child a piece of newspaper slightly larger than the frame and ask them to colour it brightly with wax crayons. Show the children how to tie a piece of wool to the frame for pulling the kite. Help them to cover the frame with the crayoned paper and fix it with tape. Finish by taping on a tail. Enjoy running with the kites, in a safe, outside area on a breezy day.

Insert pipe cleaner.
Wool or string to pull kite
Wool

Display

Use wallpaper to make a background of sky and clouds for displaying the kites after they have been used. Cover a large board with black paper and put up the toy portraits with a sign to explain the toys are part of the 'Bring and swap sale'. Display the toys on large, covered boxes nearby. Encourage the children to match the toys with their portraits.

Bringing It All Together - The Bring and Swap Sale

The Bring and Swap Sale is an ideal way for the children to appreciate some of the benefits of recycling. As they enjoy playing with toys, that their friends no longer want, they will discover that one reason for taking care of possessions is so that they may be recycled.

Preparation

At the start of the topic tell carers about the forthcoming Bring and Swap Sale. Provide ideas for the types of toys that are desired. Explain that the toys will be for children to play with, during the toy week. Also, tell the carers that on the sale day each child will be allowed to select a toy to take home. Say that further swapping days will take place in the future so that the most popular toys can be re-swapped later to give the maximum number of children the chance to play with the toys. Explain that the toys for swapping need to be in good condition.

Provide postcard sized pieces of scrap card for the children to decorate and write their names. These will be the tickets for selecting a toy. The number of tickets required will depend on the number of toys that are available for swapping.

On the swapping day set out similar toys in areas to be looked after by an adult helper. Place a card in each place to indicate the number of children that may play there. Stick a coloured label on each toy to avoid the group's usual toys being swapped! Also ensure, that the adult is aware of which are the swapping toys.

The Bring and Swap Sale

Dependent upon the number and type of toys donated the Bring and Swap Sale is likely to need one to two hours. Show the children the toys that are available in each area. Explain that first everyone is going to enjoy playing with the toys and then, at the end, they will all have the opportunity to select one toy to take home.

As you explain the areas show the number cards. Ask how many children may go in the area and then ask for volunteers. Involve the children in counting for each area. Ask the adult helpers to assist the children when needed but to allow them to play independently. Ensure that the children have the opportunity to play in a number of areas. At the end, gather all the children together. Invite the children to talk about the things they have learnt over the recycling topic and, also, what they have enjoyed playing with. Place the name cards in a basket and ask an adult helper to select one. Identify the child and invite him/her to choose a toy. Continue until all the children have made their choices.

Finish by singing, to the tune of Frère à Jacque:

We recycle, We recycle.
Why don't you? Why don't you?
Help care for our world, Help care for our world.
Recycle, Recycle.

Resources

Resources to collect:

- Unwanted, clean clothes, picture books, toys and games
- Fluorescent tabards
- Safe broken toys and ones that have missing pieces
- Plastic carriers and 'bags for life' (NB Check that they have safety air holes.)
- Plastic bottles with lids, yogurt pots, tubs etc.
- Telephone and cash register
- Long cardboard tubes
- Junk mail envelopes
- Cress seeds and fruit pips
- Set of traditional, wooden, Russian dolls
- Beanbags and balls

Everyday resources:

- Large and small boxes including cereal packets and shoe boxes
- Papers and cards of different weights, colours and textures e.g. sugar, tissue, silver and shiny papers corrugated card, etc.
- Paint, different sized paint brushes and a variety of paint mixing containers
- A variety of drawing and colouring pencils, crayons, pastels, felt pens etc.
- Glue and scissors
- Additional decorative and finishing materials such as sequins, foils, glitter, tinsel, shiny wool and threads, beads, pieces of textiles, parcel ribbon
- Table covers
- Lolly sticks, match sticks and off-cuts of wood
- Malleable materials such as play-dough
- Playground chalk
- Masking tape

All of the following books were available from leading booksellers at the time of writing. When planning for the topic, however, look through the books already within your setting. It is likely that you will find good alternatives to the suggested books.

Books for children

- *The Jolly Postman* series by Janet and Allan Ahlberg (Heinemann)
- *A Dark, Dark Tale* by Ruth Brown (Red Fox)
- *Dear Zoo* by Rod Campbell (Campbell Books Ltd)

- *The Smartest Giant* in Town by Julia Donaldson (Macmillan)
- *Goldilocks and the Three Bears* (any version)
- *The Old Bear* series by Jane Hissey (Red Fox)
- *Mog's Box* by Helen Nicholl and Jan Pieńkowski (Puffin)
- *Harry and the Bucketful of Dinosaurs* by Ian Whybrow (Puffin)
- *Harry and the Robots* by Ian Whybrow (Puffin)

Books for planning

For additional ideas linking with the 'Recycling' theme see the following titles within the Planning for Learning Series (Step Forward Publishing):

- Clothes
- Homes and Houses (Week 5: Gardens – Gives instructions for origami tulips)
- Shapes (Week 5: Boxes)
- Toys
- What are things made from?

The Early Years Foundation Stage, Setting the Standards for Learning, Development and Care for children from birth to five, Department for Education and Skills

Songs

- *Okki-tokki-unga Action Songs for Children* chosen by Beatrice Harrop, Linda Friend and David Gadsby (A & C Black Ltd)

Collecting Evidence of Children's Learning

Monitoring children's development is an important task. Keeping a record of children's achievements, interests and learning styles will help you to see progress and will draw attention to those who are having difficulties for some reason. If a child needs additional professional help, such as speech therapy, your records will provide valuable evidence.

Records should be the result of collaboration between group leaders, parents and carers. Parents should be made aware of your record keeping policies when their child joins your group. Show them the type of records you are keeping and make sure they understand that they have an opportunity to contribute. As a general rule, your records should form an open document. Any parent should have access to records relating to his or her child. Take regular opportunities to talk to parents about children's progress. If you have formal discussions regarding children about whom you have particular concerns, a dated record of the main points should be kept.

Keeping it manageable

Records should be helpful in informing group leaders, adult helpers and parents and always be for the benefit of the child. The golden rule is to keep them simple, manageable and useful.

Observations will basically fall into three categories:

- Spontaneous records: Sometimes you will want to make a note of observations as they happen e.g. a child is heard counting cars accurately during a play activity, or is seen to play collaboratively for the first time.
- Planned observations: Sometimes you will plan to make observations of children's developing skills in their everyday activities. Using the learning

opportunity identified for an activity will help you to make appropriate judgments about children's capabilities and to record them systematically.

To collect information:

- talk to children about their activities and listen to their responses;
- listen to children talking to each other;
- observe children's work such as early writing, drawings, paintings and 3D models. (Keeping photocopies or photographs is sometimes useful.)

Sometimes you may wish to set up 'one off' activities for the purposes of monitoring development. Some groups at the beginning of each term, for example, ask children to write their name and to make a drawing of themselves to record their progressing skills in both co-ordination and observation. Do not attempt to make records following every activity!

Reflective observations:

It is useful to spend regular time reflecting on the children's progress. Aim to make some comments about each child each week.

Informing your planning

Collecting evidence about children's progress is time consuming and it is important that it is useful. When you are planning, use the information you have collected to help you to decide what learning opportunities you need to provide next for children. For example, a child who has poor pencil or brush control will benefit from more play with dough or construction toys to build the strength of hand muscles.

Example of recording chart

Name: Connie Sparks		D.O.B. 31.1.04			Date of entry: 13.9.07	
Term	**Personal, Social and Emotional Development**	**Communication, Language and Literacy**	**Problem Solving, Reasoning and Numeracy**	**Knowledge and Understanding of the World**	**Physical Development**	**Creative Development**
ONE	Happy to say good-bye to mother. Enjoys both independent & collaborative play. 20.9.07. LBS	Enjoying listening to and retelling stories – excellent memory for details and phrases. Can write first name and simple CVC words. Good pencil grip. 2.10.07.CCM	Is able to say numbers to ten and to count accurately five objects. Recognises and names squares and circles. EHL 5/11/07	Very eager to ask questions always wants to know 'Why?' Loves to carry out experiments. Able to distinguish and name materials. Keen to use magnets. 16.10.07 LSS	Very flexible. Can balance on one leg. Loved miming going to a recycling centre. Does not like the feel of play dough. 16.10.07. SJS	Made a wonderful sock buddy. Loves glitter and glue! Enjoys painting and particularly when mixing own colours. Not keen to get hands messy. Will not use finger paints. 16.1.2.07 REL
TWO						
THREE						

Skills overview of six-week plan

Week	Topic Focus	Personal, Social and Emotional Development	Communication, Language and Literacy	Problem Solving, Reasoning and Numeracy	Knowledge and Understanding of the World	Physical Development	Creative Development
1	What can we recycle?	Showing interest Understanding what is right and wrong	Listening Writing Extending vocabulary	Counting Sorting Comparing Recognising and describing shapes Using positional language	Making observations Comparing Talking Selecting tools and techniques Constructing	Moving with control and imagination Aiming and throwing Showing awareness of space	Role-play Collage Painting
2	Recycling paper	Maintaining attention Selecting resources independently	Listening Responding to stories Writing Role-play	Counting Comparing Recognising shapes	Comparing Describing Investigating Asking questions	Handling objects with control and safely Using small equipment	Painting Sticking Collage
3	Recycling boxes	Speaking Initiating ideas Considering consequences Selecting resources independently	Writing Listening and responding to stories Collecting rhyming words	Sorting Counting Recognising numbers Recognising and describing shapes	Comparing Investigating Asking questions Constructing Using ICT	Moving with control and co-ordination Using small equipment	Collage Sticking Using puppets
4	Recycling plastic	Understand what is right and wrong and why Considering consequences	Using phonic knowledge to write words Speaking	Counting Recognising numbers Comparing capacities	Observing Comparing Asking questions Selecting tools and techniques Constructing Recording	Moving with control and co-ordination Throwing, catching and aiming	Role-play Making models Making and playing instruments Singing Printing
5	Recycling clothes	Dressing and undressing independently Collaborating Taking turns Showing emotions	Responding to a story Writing Speaking	Counting Recognising numbers Using the language for addition and subtraction Sorting by size	Investigating Observing Talking Selecting tools and techniques	Moving with imagination Using small and large equipment Throwing, and aiming	Cutting and sticking Painting Using puppets
6	Recycling toys and the 'Bring and Swap sale'	Understand what is right and wrong and why	Speaking Listening Responding to a story	Making patterns Comparing Using the language of shape, size and position	Asking questions Talking Selecting tools and techniques Finding out about past events Constructing	Using small equipment and malleable materials	Painting Making models Role-play

Practical Pre-School

Planning for Learning through Recycling

23

Home links

The theme of recycling lends itself to useful links with children's homes and families. Through working together children and adults gain respect for each other and build comfortable and confident relationships.

Establishing Partnerships

- Keep parents informed about the topic of 'Recycling' and the themes for each week. By understanding the work of the group, parents will enjoy the involvement of contributing ideas, time and resources.
- Photocopy the parent's page for each child to take home. Prepare a list of books, toys etc. that the group would like to collect, to go with the letter to be sent out in week 1.
- Invite friends, child minders and families to share in the Bring and Swap Sale.

Visiting Enthusiasts

- Invite adults to talk, to the group, about shopping in charity shops, the importance of recycling and how composting works. Carers could also show the group

toys that they have taken care of, that were part of their childhoods.

Resource Requests

- Catalogues, greetings cards, colour supplement magazines, wallpaper, wrapping paper, fabric, wool, and shiny materials are invaluable for collage work and a wide range of interesting activities.
- Ask parents to donate unwanted:
  Children's clothing including clean socks, Wellington boots, dressing up clothes etc.;
  Safe broken toys/games and ones with missing pieces;
  Toys in good condition for the book bags and the Bring and Swap Sale;
  Picture books – fiction and non-fiction;
  Clean plastic pots, tubs, bottles, lids;
  Re-sealable book-sized bags;
  Envelopes e.g. from junk mail;
  Boxes.

The Bring and Swap Sale

- It is always useful to have extra adults at times such as the Bring and Swap Sale.
- Involve them in helping to organise the activities and in playing with the children as they take responsibility for a given area.